THUMPER

THE MUSINGS OF A WEST HIGHLAND TERRIER

Translated into Doggerel

by

PATIENCE STRONG

Frederick Muller

First published in Great Britain in 1984 by Frederick Muller

Frederick Muller is an imprint of Muller, Blond & White Limited,
55/57 Great Ormond Street, London, WC1N 3HZ.

British Library Cataloguing in Publication Data

Strong, Patience
Thumper.
I. Title
821′.912 PR6037.T847

ISBN 0–584–11116–9

Printed and bound in Great Britain by
R. J. Acford, Chichester, Sussex.

CONTENTS

PHOTOGRAPHS OF THUMPER

by

Doris & Ronald Hemsley

Come to think of it

When you come to think of it,
        It's really not quite fair,
I have a tail and teeth,
        I have a coat of curly hair.
I have a tongue but cannot speak
        Or sing or have a chat.
I ask you – is it fair?
        How would you like to be like that?

I cannot stand up for myself
        Because I cannot say
Good morning or good afternoon,
        Or even plain good day.
I don't suppose you stop to think
        Just what it is to be
Tongue-tied in a room of people
        Talking about me.

What they do not realise is this:
    I may be dumb
But I can think. Oh yes I can.
    By night and day thoughts come
Rushing in and rushing round
    Inside my little head
Wondering and pondering
    On what is done and said.

Once inside the cottage door
    I'm safe, I'm home, I'm there,
Back where I belong. I'm happy
    With the Boss to share
Our cosy room. And even though
    He often sits all day
Behind the daily paper
    And is really miles away,

I'm on guard, for that's my job,
    So there we are: we two,
Contemplating all the things
    We know we ought to do,
Enjoying every moment
    Till the Boss quite suddenly
Switches on the talk-machine
    Then . . . exit harmony.

A voice breaks in from somebody
        Who did not knock or ring,
But in he bursts excitedly
        Some silly song to sing.
I rise and turn my back on him
        To close up eyes and ears,
Pretending to be deaf and dim
        And blind: just bored to tears.

But such is life . . . You can't expect that things throughout the day.
        Will work out as you plan them all the while and all the way.
But perhaps there is a compensation for my lack.
        I can listen even though I cannot answer back
And sometimes I'm inclined to think as through the years I go
        It's better to listen than to talk because you never know
How much trouble you avoid and how much worrying
        You save yourself by lying doggo – quietly listening.

Waiting for the turn off

My ticket to heaven

This is how I love to rest
        Between the shoes that I love best,
Underneath the Boss's chair
        In my place, I squeeze in there
Where Boss sits reading quietly,
        There's always room enough for me.

At last the visitors have gone
        So let the evening hours roll on,
For what on earth could equal this?
        This is Heaven, this is bliss.
Some good angel passed this way
        And left me a ticket with nothing to pay,
A ticket to heaven whenever I choose
        To nestle between those two brown shoes.

Some are eager to walk in space,
    Anxious to fly to some far-away place,
A mountain to climb or a desert to cross
    But all I want is to be with Boss.
I'm safe when under his chair I lie
    Contented to let the world go by,
Never fidgeting to roam
    Very far from my own good home.

Here lives my master and my friend,
    He's the beginning and the end.
Between his feet I love to rest
    In my warm and secret nest,
My corner of the universe,
    My silver key, my golden purse,
The gilded ticket that I possess
    Admitting me to happiness.

This ticket I must not mislay,
    The ticket that takes me all the way
From the babble of the news
    To my hide-away between the shoes,
Falling over the edge of sleep
    Into a well that's dark and deep,
Sinking into a cozy haze
    Dropping into a dozy daze,
Waking to find that I'm all at sea
    As to who is who and who is me.

Then back I snuggle to settle again
    In the cave that has no windowpane,
But a single star in the dark I see
    Leading to nowhere and nobody.
Without a compass or a boat
    Out through a mist of dreams I float,
Wishes like fishes go flashing by,
    I cannot catch them though I try.

Boss turns a page. The paper rustles
    Up he gets and off he bustles,
Saying "Come on, out we go,
    Best foot forward. Half a mo',
While I look for stick and hat
    I feel like food, a snack and a chat".
At first it's difficult to adjust
    But when Boss whistles – go I must.

I'm ready too – yet dreams cling so
    Boss never guesses. He cannot know
From what far country I have come
    As a sleepy soldier follows the drum.
I'm still in a world of fantasy,
    But Thumper I am, and Thumper must be
Even though summoned from a snooze
    In my Shangri-la between the shoes.

This is the way I like to be

The funny side

People know about Cheshire cats grinning from ear to ear
But seldom or maybe never do they ever chance to hear
A story about a laughing dog, for nobody ever heard
Of chuckling pugs or giggling pekes, it would be
too absurd.

But I tell you dogs do laugh, they do without a doubt.
I keep a straight face when amused, I laugh inside,
not out.
Only the other morning, how I laughed! I nearly died
Trying to keep my sense of humour bottled up inside,

As I watched a girl go by endeavouring to cope
With a pony and a donkey on a length of rope.
Laugh! You should have seen them, it *was* a funny sight:
Ten good legs between them and they couldn't get
it right.

There they were, the three of them, they really hadn't a clue.
    I'd have loved to show them what my four small legs
        could do.
But I was hidden behind the gate, observing helplessly
    This muddle of non-co-operation, this country comedy.

So back I went to the cottage, enjoying once again
    The joke of donkey, girl and pony milling around
        my brain.
Seeing the funny side, and oh how funny life can be,
    Even though you're outside the circle of humanity.

Just a spectator, a mere observer, peeping through the gate,
Watching the carnival pass, unable to communicate
But coming to the conclusion that it's all a mystery
And there's more than meets the eye as far as I can see.

There is something behind it all that no-one can explain.
Something behind the mix-up of the pleasure and
the pain,
Something incredible, something wonderful, something too
much for me
I'll be content to wait at the gate, laughing inwardly.

It's enough to make a dog laugh

It's always a wonderful day

Boss is very weather-conscious,
    First thing every day
He makes for the barometer
    To see what it will say.
Lovely weather on the way
    Or will a thunderstorm
Spoil it all and turn to grey
    The blue sky, clear and warm?

Will the wind get up or drop
    What is it going to be?
People never seem to stop
    Asking anxiously.
Worrying and wondering
    At the windowpane
Will the sun a fine day bring?
    Or are we in for rain?

Human bipeds fret and fuss
        When feet get wet outdoors,
Hurrying off to find a bus
        While I, with four good paws
Revel in the fun of pavements,
        Streaming with the rain.
Lucky me, a mere four-legger . . .
        Why should I complain?

I don't have to wear a mac,
        I love to feel upon my back
Water falling pit-a-pat . . .
        No, I'm not afraid of that.
But two-leggers have to go
        Running helter skelter
In and out and round about
        Looking for a shelter.

Their umbrellas they unfold,
    So afraid of catching cold.
It's sad to see the human race
    In decline. Such a disgrace,
Compared with my four-legged breed.
    They never start complaining,
Rushing home in a stampede,
    Just because it's raining.

Could there be a greater thrill
    Than running down a lane
When the heavens overspill
    With lots of lovely rain.
A lane where dimpled puddles lie
    And ditches, as you scamper by,
Like silver ribbons, catch the eye
    Under hedges, thick and high.
This is life at its best, say I
    Scurrying under a thundery sky.

Thumper looking at the barometer

The unfortunate incident

I'm glad I'm only what I am
    A little chap, that's me.
Friendly, docile as a lamb
    As anyone can see.
Except when strangers hover near
    And disregard my bark
Which means it is forbidden here
    To overstep the mark.

One friendly nip upon the heel
    Will prove who's master. Away they steal
Understanding the answer's "No!"
    One quick nip and away they go.

The guardian of the front door

But one sad day, I'm ashamed to tell,
    A lady came and rang the bell.
Up and out I sprang to see
    Who the visitor could be.
She stooped to pat me on the head.
    "What a dear little thing!" she said.
I saw red. I was not amused.
    Humiliated and confused,
I snapped a tiny bite or two
    At the pointed end of her polished shoe.

Then out came Boss: the feathers flew!
    What happened next I never knew
For I was bundled off inside,
    My indignation there to hide.

But after all, what is a bite?
    I was on guard, I had the right
To fight for all I hold most dear.
    We do not want intruders here.

But I never hold a grudge –
    Who am I to sit as judge? –
So I'll dismiss the whole affair
    Pretending that I do not care,
Regarding this trivial event
    As an unfortunate incident.

Just waiting

Waiting, waiting, always waiting; often it's a bore
    When you do not know exactly what you're waiting for.
But at least you get a chance to rake around your mind,
    Sorting one thing from another. Problems you may find,
But many riddles I unravel, standing still as stone,
    Even though with half my mind I'm dreaming of a bone.

Come to think of it – how much time do people spend
                                                            each day
    Waiting for something they think they want to help them
                                                            on their way?
A doctor's prescription, a train, a bus, a letter or a call,
    Only to find they never really needed it at all.
What is life but learning this one lesson: how to wait,
    That's what I wonder tethered to a railing or a gate.

Just waiting for something to turn up

I submit. I have no choice. So then I try to say
    This is a test of patience. It's my lesson for the day.
Minds like houses should be tended daily, aired and swept,
    Where no murky corners for a grievance can be kept.
Waiting times in lonely spaces should be used to bring
    Light into the dusty places, changing everything.

Many matters can be settled when you're left alone,
    Left in peace to straighten out the muddle – on your own.
Jagged edges smoothed away until they match and fit,
    Tangles disentangled thread by thread and bit by bit.
Sweeping cobwebs from the windows, letting in the sun,
    That's what life is all about when all is said and done.

I spin this sad old, bad old world when I am ruminating,
    Upside down and inside out while it is still rotating,
Till I turn it right side up, the future contemplating.
    Many problems can be solved as you are cogitating.
How to work the magic of the thing incredible.
    How to do what looks to you as nigh impossible.
How to be just me and to perform the miracle,
    While waiting.

Soap gets in your eyes

When I come to think of it, I used to dread the day
When I was due to have a bath, and tried to hide away,
Hoping it would be forgotten on the roundabout
Of comings and of goings up and down and in and out.

Every Wednesday morning off the bus comes Muriel
To tidy up the cottage, leaving behind a smell
Of disinfectant, soap and polish, wax and lavender,
The homely, healthy smells that I associate with her.

Round the oak-beamed rooms she rushes with a feather mop,
And with a brush and pan up from the bottom to the top
She does the stairs, then off she goes to catch the bus at two,
Leaving behind a place that looks all shiny, fresh
and new.

I'm very fond of Muriel because she understands
What I feel because I have no fingers and no hands.
Without a word she seems to know the things I cannot tell:
How I feel and what I want – she knows, dear Muriel.

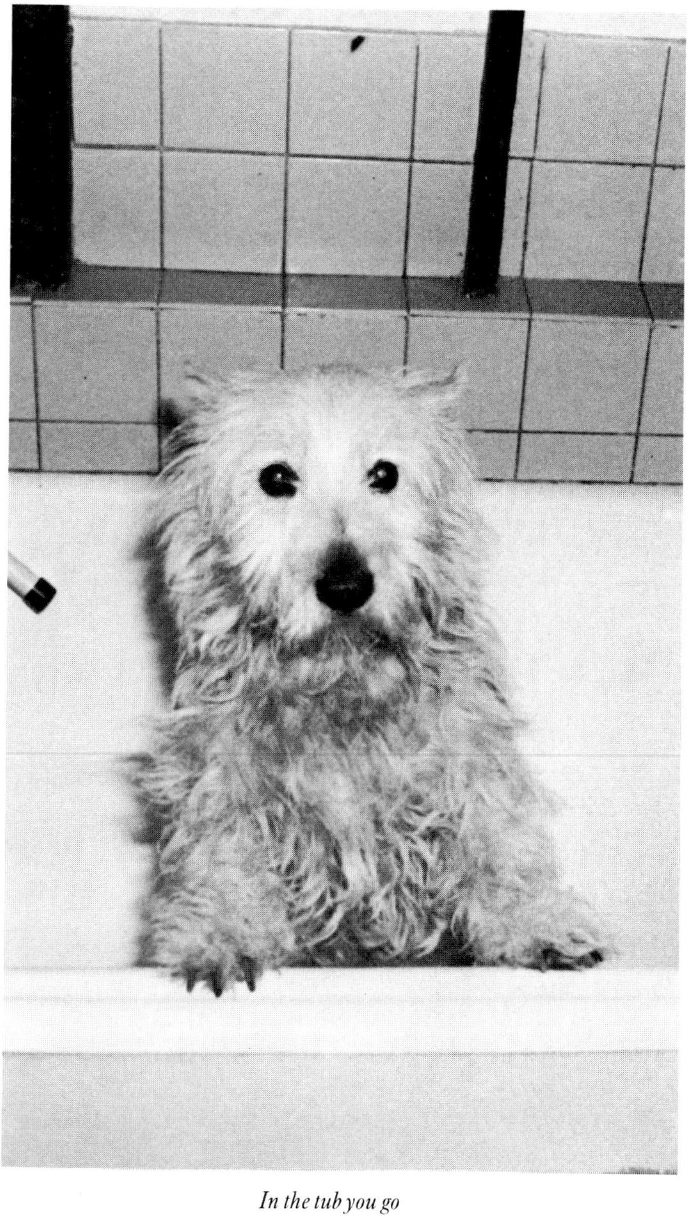

In the tub you go

Then one morning in she came and said to me, "Ho – ho!
You look as if you need a bath, so in the tub you go . . .
And I'll have no nonsense." So she scooped me up the stairs.
I submitted, for I had been taken unawares,
And dumped into a foamy bubbly bath to romp about
Then scrubbed and rubbed and combed, I felt a swell.
Without a doubt
I'd needed it, but when I saw the water round me rise
I was scared, remembering that soap gets in your eyes.

But I confess I'm looking forward to the next big dip
Now I know what to expect. When taking off I slip
Plonk into the water. First I floundered in a flap
Frightened by the rushing of the running of the tap.
Very soon I found that I could lie, or stand, or sit,
And it's easy once you really get the hang of it,
So long as you remember what the experts all advise:
Never ever to forget that soap gets in your eyes.

The very peculiar day

Thinking of it every way
  It was a very peculiar day.
It had a beginning – and ending too
  But it had no middle. I never knew
Why the time passed all too soon
  On the day that had no afternoon.

First thing that morning I could see
  Boss was busy as a bee.
He was expecting company
  Trevor and Sonia for tea
Daughter and son-in-law. Family.

Then I remembered that other day
  When I was suddenly whisked away.
Trevor, it seemed, at sight of me
  Sneezed. They called it an allergy.
So this time I hid behind a chair
  Hoping they would not spot me there
For I was curious to see
  What the mystery could be –
They'd put something upon the floor
  Between the window and the door.

Cramped as I was in restricted space
        A look I took from my hiding place
Astonished to see a baby's cot
        Blue as a new forget-me-not.
And under a frilly cover spread
        There rested the little golden head
Of a tiny human mite
        There on a pillow, snowy white.

Then a small hand I espied.
        At that I quite forgot to hide,
For alive it seemed to be,
        Waving across the room to me!
Mad with excitement I rushed about
        Then up came Boss to carry me out
On the kitchen rug to lie
        Till our visitors said goodbye.

LAROUSSE
OXFORD
in the History of the Nation
IMAGE of CANADA

Banished

Later I stood on the window sill
As the sun went down behind the hill
Watching them go through the garden gate
Hurrying, it was getting late
And, would you believe it, I saw once more
That small hand waving as before
As if to say, "Bad luck, old chap
I hope you had a lovely nap.
Just you wait a year or two
And I shall be seeing you.
Together we'll have lots of fun
Taking Grandpa for a run
Over the bridge and down the lane
Bye bye – I'll soon be back again".

Later that night I was trying to think,
There in my basket beside the sink,
Remembering that tiny hand
As I came to the edge of the Dreamy Land,
Counting the hours as they slipped away
At the end of that very peculiar day.

The old gentleman

Sooner or later, we all come to the stage
Where we start to think about the horrid question of age . . .
Sometimes when I'm on the lead out in the village street
A stranger we encounter, or an acquaintance meet
With whom Boss stops to chat, which I consider a waste of time:
So precious every moment is, to waste it is a crime.

Why should they ask how old I am? Why not "How young?" Why not?
I resent this questioning, it puts me on the spot.
"Twelve" says Boss, and there they stare, considering my span
"Quite a veteran," they remark, "a fine old gentleman!"

Busybodies I abhor. It's not their business
To wonder if I'm seven, ten or twelve, or more, or less.
I'd like to know if they with me would care to run a race.
I doubt if they could even do it at a walking pace.

Grow old gracefully, people say, if youth you can't re-call,
    But better still I'd like to ask them, why grow old at all?
If your mind rejects the image of decrepitude
    Change your mental attitude and life itself will
        be renewed,
Always hopeful, looking forward, never giving way,
    Being positive, never negative, younger every day.

Look at me, I never pay a visit to the vet.
    One day, someday, maybe . . . but it hasn't happened yet.
I'm as frisky as a pup and lively as a frog,
    Enjoying being what I am, just Thumper – me, the dog.
Daily I jump across the stream, thank goodness I still can,
    Refusing to be designated "an old gentleman".

I feel fine

The magic moment

This is really something marvellous,
Something that you could describe as almost miraculous.
To think that a dumb and ordinary creature such as me
Knows the time without the aid of clock or BBC.

How do I know it? That I cannot answer, but I know . . .
I know because I know I know. The marching minutes go
Regular as clockwork soldiers, never turning back
Always pressing on along a never-ending track.

What I know is this: that when it's near to half past five
I get the psychic message. Up I spring alert, alive.
The moment has arrived. I still am Thumper, but within
I sense the magic signal of the opening of a tin
And feel the stirring of a spirit animating me
To leap upstairs and down again in frenzied ecstasy.

Without the clanging of a gong or ringing of a bell
I know the moment now has come . . . I know, I know full well
That a feast for me is set beside the kitchen sink
Served by the hand of Boss himself. I'm a lucky dog, I think.

I dine at 5.30

I want for nothing, but still we have not solved the mystery
Of what occurs at half past five. What enters into me?
When I feel the urge to act in a wild nonsensical way,
Barking up and down the stairs at a certain time each day
Just before the striking of the clock, but who can say
How the magic works and who it is who runs the show?
But it happens, yes, it happens, I know because I know . . .
Not how to tell the time, but how to listen and to wait,
Anticipating what I hope to see upon my plate.

Crossword puzzles

Life is a series of crossword puzzles. With breakfast
cleared away
Boss gets down to the solving of the puzzle for the day,
Which occupies his whole attention, like a drug it clings
To his mind, obliterating ordinary things.
Hour by hour he cogitates the puzzle to complete,
While I lie patient and expectant, waiting at his feet
Making sure he's not disturbed, put out in any way . . .
The puzzle must be tackled, fought and finished, come
what may.

But things become a little strained when Muriel appears,
Standing the hoover in the corner, sometimes near
to tears,
She pleads, "Please may I come and do the carpet. Quick
I'll be."
Eyeing the papers spread around us disapprovingly,
Making us feel we're holding up the run of the routine,
Casting the shadow of a cloud on our domestic scene.

Boss pretends not to hear

Then boss says, "Come on Thumper, later on it will be done.
The battle of the hoover's lost before it has begun."
So off we go defeated, but we knew how it would be.
It always ends like this . . . but I was laughing inwardly
Because it means a ramble round the village green for me
And I would never miss so good an opportunity.

All too soon we would be back where Boss could try once more
To find the puzzling clue to words that must be
hunted for,
Until a sigh of satisfaction from the chair is heard
And I know that he at last has found the missing word.
That restores his self-esteem and sends him on his way
Rejoicing in the finding of the word that makes his day.

In and out

When I think of these two-leggers, foolish they appear
As they shoot off from the earth into the upper sphere,
Spouting smoke and fumes and germs, intruding shamelessly
Into the starry spaces where they have no right to be.

Restless creatures, always on the go, they can't relax,
No wonder that their bodies and their brains they overtax
Speeding here and speeding there, up, down, in and out
Nervous wrecks before they know what life is all about.

You'd think they'd take a tip from me, relaxing on the floor
Stretched out like a cat, the nervous system to restore.
At any moment I can flop and let life have its way
Repairing and renewing me, and this is why I stay
Well prepared for all that comes and always fighting fit,
Knowing that I can cope – whatever comes, I deal with it.

When they get out in the air it's not for racing round
To run for fun, to throw a ball, or up a bank to bound,
But just to do the boring thing of looking for a shop
Their never-ending search for food goes on and on
non-stop.
First it's breakfast, then it's lunch, then all the fuss of tea,
Then it's supper or late dinner . . . that's no life for me.

At any moment I can flop and relax

The best part of a holiday

The best part of a holiday, I think it every year,
    Is when it's nearly over and the time is very near
For packing bags and setting off to where we both belong,
    Back to our corner in the country. Am I right or wrong?

That's where I belong and that is where I wish we'd stay . . .
    All this packing and unpacking just to get away!
Whoever wants a holiday travelling near or far?
    Why can't we be left in peace to stay just where we are?

Here, I'm trotted out each day upon the Grand Parade
    Or taken to the water's edge, to wallow or to wade . . .
Such a bore! I'm sorry for the dog who has to be
    Paraded on the Esplanade. It's not the life for me.

I am nobody's seaside pet. I'm country, born and bred.
Through a meadow by a stream I love to rush ahead
Scrambling down the banks where rushes quiver in the breeze
And a little river runs between the willow trees.

I must not make comparisons: they're odious, so they say.
Let every man and every creature go his own sweet way.
Some to sit on pebbles waiting for the tide to turn,
Some to sit beside the cosy hearth where birch logs burn,
Knowing that outside there is the country to explore!
The great green world that beckons from beyond the old front door.

Goodbye to the railings

Now I know it's time to go, a kinder view I take
Of the balcony and the steps, if just for old time's sake.
Sentimental I become when comes the final day.
Perhaps because when getting older one can never say
Whether you will pass this way again, though year by year
We have had a holiday, always staying here.

But thoughts are never on the leash, for they are free to roam
Everywhere and anywhere. But when you're
heading home
It really is the nicest part of any holiday
So goodbye to the railings; here we come, we're on
our way!

Lost

Never, no, never shall I forget the day when I was lost.
What a sad little word that is! I've been tumbled
and tossed
On the stormy seas of fortune, but I've kept afloat
Since that day when I, like baby Moses in a boat,
Landed up on Charlotte's doorstep in a basket laid.
That was a long, long, time ago when first the world
was made.

Many things she taught me in that hillside bungalow,
Where around the windowpanes red roses used to
grow . . .
Happy days, what walks we had, we two! Then suddenly
Charlotte was Mrs Boss, and then we two became
we three.
But came a day when our dear Charlotte was taken down
the lane
In an ambulance, never ever to return again.

So Boss with me beside him crossed the borderline of Kent,
Facing the future together to the next new world we went.
So here we are and still together, never more to roam
The old, old cottage seemed to say, "Come in for here is home."

A long way back I've wandered in my effort to recall,
That's what comes of thinking back to the saddest day of all:
The day when I was lost, the day I slipped out through the gate,
Across the road, my favourite corner to investigate,
Where two streams meet and there's a weir that makes a splashing sound.
I never have the chance to linger when we're homeward bound,
So I seized the opportunity, but off the main path strayed . . .
Too late I realised what a serious blunder I had made.

Back once more where I belong

At last tired out I gave up looking, feeling very sad
    To think I'd lost my home, the nicest home I'd ever had.
Then a miracle happened, a face that well I knew,
    The rosy face of Freddie, with his Airedale, came in view.
Up I got and raced towards him and he lifted me
    Into his big strong arms – and was I thankful there to be!
Knowing he would carry me and take me home again.
    Many times when Boss and I were walking down the lane
We had met him but that evening I was glad that he
    Had decided to walk that way, and so to rescue me.
Boss was at the gate and in I ran, relieved to be
    Back once more where I belonged . . . oh silly,
        lucky, me!

But if I lived a hundred years, I never should forget
    How lonely I felt as I watched the sinking sun until it set,
And on the sky the stars like golden buttons were embossed
    At the end of the saddest day of all, the day when I
        was lost.

Sentenced to silence

These two-leggers wag their tongues all day
    Nattering, chattering, even though there's nothing left
        to say.
Day and night they keep it up and never do they flag –
    Conversations ramble on, and seldom limp or lag.
It is quite surprising when you come to think of it,
    Never pausing to take a breath or just to rest a bit.

How I wonder how they'd like to change and be like me,
    Never speaking a word, compelled in company dumb
        to be.
Just listening at the receiving end,
    Never exchanging confidences even with a friend.

Now I come to think of it, with all this crime about
It wouldn't be a bad idea to let the convicts out,
And send them home with muzzles on, in silence to remain
Till they'd served their sentences. They'd never risk again
Such a punishment to endure. Perhaps reformed they'd be,
Just by being made to sit and listen quietly.

Made to remember animals always had this cross to bear.
They can hear but cannot speak, and so they cannot share
Their thoughts with anybody, any time or anywhere,
Though it's often seemed to me to be a bit unfair.
But this would teach them lessons in the way they should behave,
And think of all the money that the government would save!

The more I come to think of it, the more I think that I
Should have some sort of silver medal round my neck to tie,
In recognition of the fact that I, with no degree,
Had thought up something that should take its place in history.
Many a judge would be relieved if such a thing could be
Passed by law to be the universal remedy.

For every crime committed let the prisoner decide
Whether he'll go to jail or at his own address abide,
Muzzled like an animal in comfort at home to dwell . . .
Or effaced in prison, in disgrace, cooped in a cell.
The law they say is complicated, like a monkey puzzle,
But how simple it could be: the prison or the muzzle.

Never uttering a word

Common dog sense

Come to think of it, day after day and year after year after year
Men make their legs work all the time – the strain must be severe,
Climbing, skating, jogging, jumping, always on the go,
Cycling, kneeling, dancing, walking, running to and fro.

Now and then I watch them on the television screen,
Olympic runners, medal winners, always fit and keen.
But I pity them, poor things, for me they'd never beat . . .
How could they compete, with only two big clumsy feet?

I have twice as many legs and four efficient paws.
Like a streak of lightning I could beat them all because
I was made for speed, for swift pursuit and giving chase.
But these, these mere two-leggers, they were made for a walker's pace.

How, I wonder, would they react to this? And could they bear
To wear a leathery collar round their necks that's always there.
As soon as I put my nose outside the door, the warnings come
"Now then Thumper, wait a minute. What's the hurry, chum?".

How was I to get down?

As for coping with stairs, two-leggers have the
advantage there.
I have four little legs to manage, it's not really fair.
Four little legs to co-ordinate, four little legs to train,
To carry me up a flight of stairs, and carry me
down again.

I was bungalow born and bred so stairs to me were new
Until I came to Sussex. There I met my Waterloo.
When I to the cottage came, I took one look and stopped
to stare . . .
Was I expected to fly? Oh how was I to get up there?

Then Boss, impatient, came along and carried me aloft,
Dumped me at the top and said, "Now Thumper, don't
be soft,
You've got to do it, so do it now, at once without delay . . .
Don't wait for someone to show you,
Teaching yourself is the only way."

It's always Christmas

Come to think of it, Christmas always seems to be
somewhere near.
Either it's coming or it's going. All too soon we hear:
How many days are left for shopping? How many? As if
we cared!
Christmas to me means more than cakes and crackers.
If we dared
We'd plan to keep next Christmas in a quiet and different way,
Saving the eating and the drinking for the
New Year's Day.

Christmas is out of this world. For twenty-four hours, no
more, no less
Man is lifted out of himself and into otherness.
Christmas is like a mysterious cave where precious
treasure lies.
The very pearl of life itself for the simple and the wise
Is hidden there, and only those who know the way can find
The secret path to the secret place of the Lord of
all mankind.

Cards and crackers

How do I know it? I know it because a stranger, passing
this way,
Told me the marvellous story of the Babe of
Christmas Day.
And here's another thing I know: dumb creatures came to see
The little Messiah of Bethlehem, they stood in humility
Beside the crib in the stable, where the infant Saviour lay . . .
The Prince of Peace, the world's redeemer, cradled in
the hay.

First at the stable, first at the manger before the shepherds
were there,
Donkey, oxen and lambkin standing still, as if at prayer.
Asses and camels and horses and a dove of purest white
Had come like the holy family, sheltering for the night.
Obeying the voice that bade them go, marvellous things to see
When the long-expected Jesus entered history.

You do not need a super brain these things to understand
Or to know exactly how a world like this was planned
But if a cat can look at a Queen, a dog can look at a King.
Is not all creation His? And cannot all creatures bring
An offering to the manger Throne? And could it not be
that He
A corner would keep in the Kingdom for a little chap
like me?

Every time that Christmas comes, this dream I dream again,
Waiting to see the herald angel through the windowpane.
But even if next Christmas brings no trumpets to the skies
And it's only the same old thing: parties, puddings
and pies,
Come this Christmas, or come the next, I'll go on
waiting here,
Believing, never doubting that the Christmas
drawing near
Will be the last of the Christmases; the best of all that brings
The promised return in power and glory of the King
of Kings.

Through the windowpane